Visit us at *www.kidsbooks.com*.
Volume discounts available for group purchases.

FIND FREDDIE

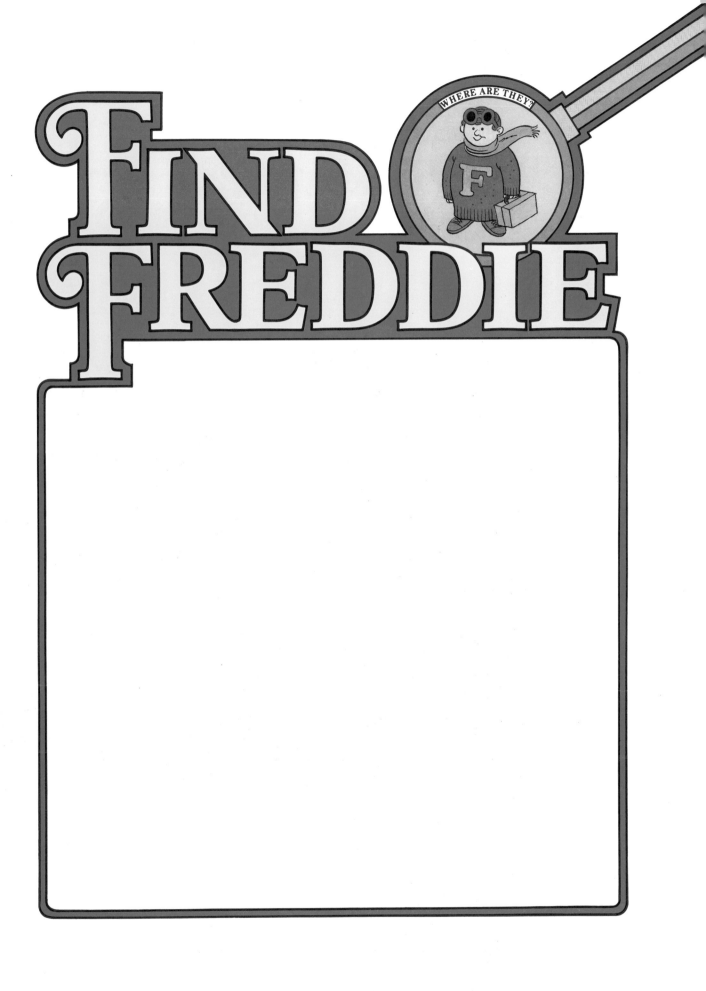

FIND FREDDIE AT HOME AND . . .

- ☐ Alligator
- ☐ Apple
- ☐ Big foot
- ☐ Bird's nest
- ☐ Boxing glove
- ☐ Bug
- ☐ Cupcake
- ☐ Deflated balloon
- ☐ Dinosaur
- ☐ 4 Drumsticks
- ☐ Eight ball
- ☐ Electric guitar
- ☐ False teeth
- ☐ Fire hydrant
- ☐ Football helmet
- ☐ Footprints
- ☐ Giant pencil
- ☐ "Goof Off" medal
- ☐ 2 Hamburgers
- ☐ Lifesaver
- ☐ 2 Locomotives
- ☐ Magnifying glass
- ☐ Mailbox
- ☐ Model plane
- ☐ Monster hand
- ☐ Mouse house
- ☐ 3 Music notes
- ☐ Paintbrush
- ☐ Ping-pong net
- ☐ "Quarantine"
- ☐ Sled
- ☐ Slice of pizza
- ☐ Snake
- ☐ Soccer ball
- ☐ 3 Speakers
- ☐ Tent
- ☐ Thermometer
- ☐ "Think Small"
- ☐ 13:15
- ☐ Top hat
- ☐ Toy car
- ☐ Tricycle
- ☐ "Yech!"
- ☐ Yo-yo

FIND FREDDIE IN SPACE AND . . .

- [ ] Alien basketball player
- [ ] Barbell
- [ ] Barber
- [ ] 2 Bats
- [ ] Bow tie
- [ ] Butterfly
- [ ] Cow
- [ ] Crayon
- [ ] Dragon
- [ ] Dunce cap
- [ ] Earmuffs
- [ ] Elephant
- [ ] 2 Feet
- [ ] Firecracker
- [ ] 2 Flying fish
- [ ] Flying horse
- [ ] Hammer
- [ ] Happy face
- [ ] 4 Hot dogs
- [ ] Igloo
- [ ] Kite
- [ ] 10 Moons
- [ ] Moviemaker
- [ ] Nose
- [ ] Owl
- [ ] P.D.
- [ ] Part of a star
- [ ] Peter Pan
- [ ] Pinocchio
- [ ] Pig
- [ ] Pizza
- [ ] Planet Earth
- [ ] Santa Claus
- [ ] Seal
- [ ] Skateboard
- [ ] Skull planet
- [ ] Space cat
- [ ] "Stairwars"
- [ ] Submarine
- [ ] Sunglasses
- [ ] Telescope
- [ ] Traffic signal
- [ ] Truck
- [ ] Tulips
- [ ] Two-headed alien

FIND FREDDIE AT THE BEACH AND . . .

- ☐ Angry dog
- ☐ Angry horse
- ☐ Bulldozer
- ☐ Caddy
- ☐ Castle
- ☐ 3 Cats
- ☐ Eskimo
- ☐ Firefighter
- ☐ 3 Football players
- ☐ Hungry fish
- ☐ Hungry lion
- ☐ 2 Ice cream cones
- ☐ Kangaroo
- ☐ Launch site
- ☐ Laundry
- ☐ Life raft
- ☐ Mailbox
- ☐ Motorcyclist
- ☐ "New Sand"
- ☐ Octopus
- ☐ Oil well
- ☐ Paint-by-number
- ☐ Panda
- ☐ Periscope
- ☐ Policeman
- ☐ "Quicksand"
- ☐ 2 Radios
- ☐ Record
- ☐ Robot
- ☐ Rock surfer
- ☐ Seahorse
- ☐ Sea serpent
- ☐ Seltzer bottle
- ☐ Singing cowboy
- ☐ Snail
- ☐ Strong wind
- ☐ 3 Tires
- ☐ Tuba player
- ☐ 6 Turtles
- ☐ Twin boys
- ☐ 8 Umbrellas
- ☐ "Used Sand"
- ☐ Very fat man
- ☐ Wet dog

FIND FREDDIE
AT SCHOOL AND...

- [ ] Apple
- [ ] Awakening monster
- [ ] Balloon
- [ ] "Ban Homework"
- [ ] Bare feet
- [ ] 2 Baseball bats
- [ ] Baton twirler
- [ ] Bowling ball
- [ ] Boy Scout
- [ ] Cake
- [ ] Cannon
- [ ] Clock setter
- [ ] Coach
- [ ] Cook
- [ ] "Disco"
- [ ] Explosion
- [ ] Fish tank
- [ ] Guitar
- [ ] Headless horseman
- [ ] Helium filled bubble gum
- [ ] Jump rope
- [ ] Lost ear
- [ ] Mouse attack
- [ ] Pumpkin
- [ ] 2 Rabbits
- [ ] 5 Report cards
- [ ] Roller skates
- [ ] Robot
- [ ] Rocket launch
- [ ] "Room To Let"
- [ ] 4 "School Closed" signs
- [ ] Secret trap door
- [ ] Ship
- [ ] 2 Sleeping students
- [ ] Snake
- [ ] Soccer practice
- [ ] Surfboard
- [ ] Tent
- [ ] Tuba
- [ ] 4 TV antennae
- [ ] Tyrannosaurus
- [ ] Water bomb
- [ ] Weightlifter

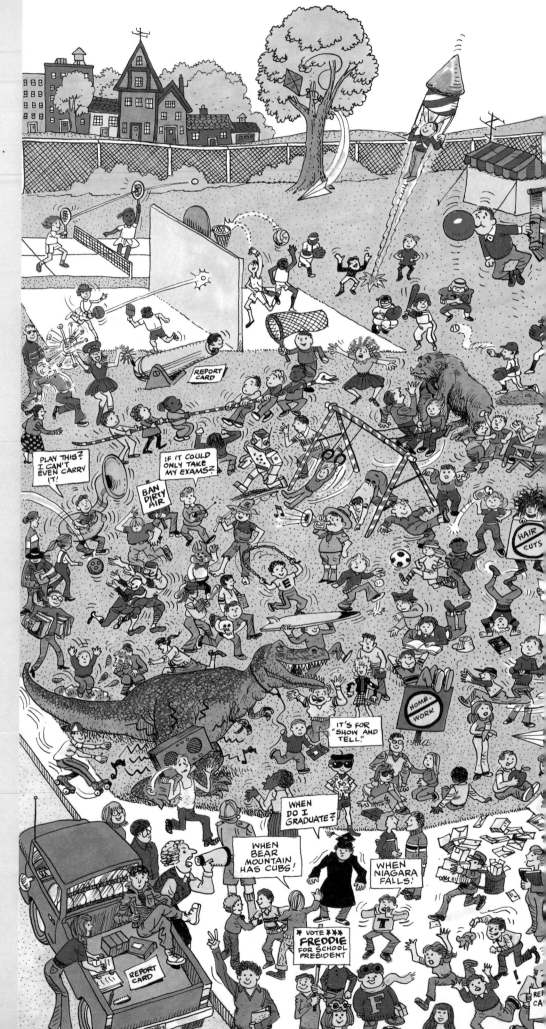

FIND FREDDIE
ON THE SCHOOL
BUS TRIP AND . . .

- [ ] Airplane
- [ ] Alligator
- [ ] Ambulance
- [ ] 5 Balloons
- [ ] Banana
- [ ] Barbershop
- [ ] Birdcage
- [ ] Boat
- [ ] "Bubble Gum Co."
- [ ] Burger-mobile
- [ ] Circus tent
- [ ] 3 Clocks
- [ ] Closed road
- [ ] Covered wagon
- [ ] Diver
- [ ] Doghouse
- [ ] Donkey
- [ ] Fish-mobile
- [ ] Garbage truck
- [ ] Gas station
- [ ] Ghost
- [ ] Horseshoe
- [ ] Hotel
- [ ] Igloo-mobile
- [ ] Jack-in-the-box
- [ ] Jellybean factory
- [ ] Lake serpent
- [ ] Library
- [ ] Locomotive
- [ ] 2 Mice
- [ ] Milk truck
- [ ] One-eyed monster
- [ ] Sailor cap
- [ ] Sandwich
- [ ] "72"
- [ ] 4 Sheep
- [ ] "Shopping Mall"
- [ ] 2 Skulls
- [ ] Sombrero
- [ ] Teepee-mobile
- [ ] Telephone
- [ ] Telescope
- [ ] Tennis racket
- [ ] Tow truck
- [ ] 2 Used tires

FIND FREDDIE IN MONSTERVILLE AND . . .

- ☐ 6 Arrows
- ☐ Bathbrush
- ☐ 13 Bats
- ☐ Ben Franklin
- ☐ Broken clock
- ☐ Broken heart
- ☐ Carrot
- ☐ Clothespin
- ☐ Cowgirl
- ☐ Daisy
- ☐ "Dead End"
- ☐ Dog
- ☐ Eye in the sky
- ☐ Flying carpet
- ☐ Garbage can
- ☐ 6 Ghosts
- ☐ "Harvard Drop-Out"
- ☐ Humpty Dumpty
- ☐ Ice cream cone
- ☐ Key
- ☐ "Kids Ahead"
- ☐ Kite
- ☐ Ladder
- ☐ Mailbox
- ☐ Mail carrier
- ☐ Ms. Transylvania
- ☐ "No Fishing"
- ☐ 3 Number 13's
- ☐ One-eyed monster
- ☐ "One way"
- ☐ Octopus
- ☐ 7 Pumpkins
- ☐ Rabbit
- ☐ Skeleton
- ☐ 8 Skulls
- ☐ Sprinkler
- ☐ Tic-tac-toe
- ☐ Truck
- ☐ TV set
- ☐ Weird doctor
- ☐ 2 Welcome mats
- ☐ Window washer
- ☐ Witch
- ☐ Young Dracula's wagon

FIND FREDDIE AT THE AIRPORT AND . . .

- ☐ Arrow
- ☐ Banana peel
- ☐ 3 Bats
- ☐ Bear
- ☐ Bird in love
- ☐ Boots
- ☐ Bride and groom
- ☐ Chicken
- ☐ Clown
- ☐ Cow
- ☐ Dart
- ☐ Dog pilot
- ☐ "Don't Fly"
- ☐ "Fly"
- ☐ Flying saucer
- ☐ 4 Fuel trucks
- ☐ Globe
- ☐ Golfer
- ☐ Hockey stick
- ☐ Horse
- ☐ "ICU2"
- ☐ Leaping lizard
- ☐ Long beard
- ☐ Luggage carrier
- ☐ "One Way"
- ☐ 3 Paper planes
- ☐ Photographer
- ☐ Pterosaur
- ☐ Rabbit
- ☐ 2 Sailboats
- ☐ Santa Claus
- ☐ Seesaw
- ☐ Sherlock Holmes
- ☐ Shooting star
- ☐ Space capsule
- ☐ "Star Wreck"
- ☐ Super hero
- ☐ Telescope
- ☐ Teepee
- ☐ 2 Unicorns
- ☐ Walnut
- ☐ Watermelon slice
- ☐ Windsock
- ☐ Winged man
- ☐ Wooden leg

FIND FREDDIE AT THE BALLPARK AND . . .

- [ ] Basketball
- [ ] 3 Beach balls
- [ ] 3 Birds
- [ ] Bone
- [ ] Boxing glove
- [ ] Bubble gum bubble
- [ ] Car
- [ ] Clothesline
- [ ] Cyclist
- [ ] 3 Dancers
- [ ] Elephant
- [ ] Fish
- [ ] Football team
- [ ] Frankenstein monster
- [ ] Ghost
- [ ] Giraffe
- [ ] Gorilla
- [ ] "Happy Section"
- [ ] 3 Hearts
- [ ] Horse
- [ ] 2 "Hot" dogs
- [ ] Lawn mower
- [ ] Lost shoe
- [ ] Mascot
- [ ] Monster hand
- [ ] 6 "No. 1" hands
- [ ] "Out" banner
- [ ] Painter
- [ ] 5 Paper airplanes
- [ ] Parachutist
- [ ] Rabbit
- [ ] Showers
- [ ] Sleeping player
- [ ] Snowman
- [ ] Tic-tac-toe
- [ ] Torn pants
- [ ] Turtle
- [ ] 4 TV cameras
- [ ] 2 TV sets
- [ ] Two-gloved fan
- [ ] 3 Umbrellas
- [ ] Uncle Sam
- [ ] Viking
- [ ] Yellow slicker

FIND FREDDIE
AT THE MUSEUM
AND . . .

- ☐ 4 Artists
- ☐ Baby crying
- ☐ 3 Bees
- ☐ Bike racer
- ☐ Bomb
- ☐ Bowler
- ☐ Boy Scout
- ☐ Cactus
- ☐ Doctor
- ☐ Dracula
- ☐ Elephant
- ☐ Escaped convict
- ☐ Fire hose
- ☐ "First Prize"
- ☐ Girl fishing
- ☐ "For Sail"
- ☐ Giant soda
- ☐ Giant whistle
- ☐ Hamburger
- ☐ Hammock
- ☐ 5 Hearts
- ☐ Jester
- ☐ Juggler
- ☐ "Last Clean
     Air"
- ☐ Man rowing
- ☐ Mirror
- ☐ Mummy
- ☐ Musician
- ☐ Peanuts
- ☐ Peanut vendor
- ☐ Photographer
- ☐ Pizza delivery
- ☐ Princess
- ☐ Rope climber
- ☐ Sand castle
- ☐ Santa Claus
- ☐ Sherlock Holmes
- ☐ "Slowsand"
- ☐ Smoke signals
- ☐ Space capsule
- ☐ Sun
- ☐ Target
- ☐ Taxi
- ☐ Telephone booth
- ☐ "Thin Ice"

FIND FREDDIE IN THE OLD WEST TOWN AND . . .

- ☐ Alien
- ☐ Bald Indian
- ☐ Banana peel
- ☐ Bearded man
- ☐ 7 Bedbugs
- ☐ Boot Hill
- ☐ 6 Cactuses
- ☐ Cat
- ☐ "Condos"
- ☐ 5 Ducklings
- ☐ Fire hydrant
- ☐ Fistfight
- ☐ Flying saucer
- ☐ "Ghost Town"
- ☐ Hand-in-a-box
- ☐ Hobo hitchhiker
- ☐ Jailbreak
- ☐ Jockey
- ☐ Lasso
- ☐ Long johns
- ☐ One-man-band
- ☐ Painted mountain
- ☐ Parking meter
- ☐ Piano player
- ☐ Piggy bank
- ☐ 3 Rabbits
- ☐ Rain cloud
- ☐ Rhinoceros
- ☐ Rocking horse
- ☐ Satellite dish
- ☐ Shark fin
- ☐ Sharpshooter
- ☐ Sheriff
- ☐ Snake
- ☐ Snowman
- ☐ Soccer ball
- ☐ Stampede
- ☐ "Tacos"
- ☐ 8 Teepees
- ☐ "Texas"
- ☐ Theater
- ☐ 2 Tombstones
- ☐ Unicorn
- ☐ Witch

FIND FREDDIE   LOOK FOR LISA   HUNT FOR HECTOR   SEARCH FOR S

HUNT FOR HECTOR
AT THE DOG HALL
OF FAME
AND ...

- ☐ Alien
- ☐ Astronaut
- ☐ Automobile
- ☐ Babe Ruff
- ☐ 2 Birds
- ☐ Boot
- ☐ "Buffalo Bull"
- ☐ Cannon
- ☐ Cat
- ☐ "Cave Dog"
- ☐ Clown
- ☐ Cook
- ☐ Doghouse
- ☐ "Down Boy"
- ☐ Elephant
- ☐ Fallen star
- ☐ Flying dog
- ☐ Football
- ☐ Ghost dog
- ☐ 2 Giant bones
- ☐ Guard dog
- ☐ Hot dog
- ☐ Husky
- ☐ Indian
- ☐ Juggler
- ☐ Kangaroo
- ☐ Man on leash
- ☐ Mirror
- ☐ Moon
- ☐ Mouse
- ☐ Napoleon
- ☐ Photographer
- ☐ Pilgrim
- ☐ Pirate flag
- ☐ Record player
- ☐ Santa hound
- ☐ Sheep
- ☐ Sherlock Bones
- ☐ Stamp
- ☐ Super hero
- ☐ Super poodle
- ☐ Target
- ☐ Tin can
- ☐ Umpire

HUNT FOR HECTOR AT DOG SCHOOL AND . . .

- ☐ A-ARF
- ☐ Artist's model
- ☐ Banana peel
- ☐ Building plans
- ☐ Cat
- ☐ Chalk
- ☐ Clipboard
- ☐ Cloud
- ☐ Comic book
- ☐ Cook
- ☐ Cork
- ☐ Crown
- ☐ 2 Dancing dogs
- ☐ Doggy bag
- ☐ Doggy bank
- ☐ Dogwood
- ☐ Dunce cap
- ☐ Eraser
- ☐ Fire hydrant
- ☐ Flying bone
- ☐ 2 Forks
- ☐ Frankendog
- ☐ Genie
- ☐ Graduate
- ☐ Hammer
- ☐ Handkerchief
- ☐ "Hi, Mom!"
- ☐ "History Of Bones"
- ☐ Hockey stick
- ☐ "How To Bark"
- ☐ Leash
- ☐ Mail carrier
- ☐ Mush
- ☐ 2 Pencils
- ☐ P.T.A.
- ☐ Roller skates
- ☐ Saw
- ☐ 2 School bags
- ☐ Scooter
- ☐ Sun
- ☐ Sunglasses
- ☐ Triangle
- ☐ T-square

HUNT FOR HECTOR
AMONG THE DOG
CATCHERS
AND . . .

- ☐ Airplane
- ☐ Alien
- ☐ "Arf"
- ☐ Balloon
- ☐ Barber pole
- ☐ Carrots
- ☐ 5 Cats
- ☐ 3 Chimneys
- ☐ 3 Dog bowls
- ☐ 7 Dog catchers
- ☐ Doghouse
- ☐ Drums
- ☐ Firedogs
- ☐ 4 Fire hydrants
- ☐ Fisherdog
- ☐ 2 Flagpoles
- ☐ Flying saucer
- ☐ Gas mask
- ☐ 2 Howling dogs
- ☐ "Keep Things Clean"
- ☐ Mailbox
- ☐ Manhole cover
- ☐ 9 Police dogs
- ☐ 2 Restaurants
- ☐ Roadblock
- ☐ Rock and roll dog
- ☐ Santa dog
- ☐ Scout
- ☐ Shower
- ☐ Slice of pizza
- ☐ Streetlight
- ☐ 4 Super hero dogs
- ☐ Telephone
- ☐ Trail of money
- ☐ Trash can
- ☐ Tree
- ☐ 10 Trucks
- ☐ Turtle
- ☐ TV antenna
- ☐ TV camera
- ☐ Umbrella

HUNT FOR HECTOR
WHERE THE RICH
AND FAMOUS DOGS
LIVE AND . . .

- [ ] Admiral
- [ ] Alligator
- [ ] Artist
- [ ] Bank
- [ ] "Big Wheel"
- [ ] Bird bath
- [ ] Blimp
- [ ] Bone chimney
- [ ] Candle
- [ ] Castle
- [ ] Cat
- [ ] 2 Cooks
- [ ] Crown
- [ ] Dog fish
- [ ] Dog flag
- [ ] Dog prince statue
- [ ] 2 Dog-shaped bushes
- [ ] Door dog
- [ ] Fat dog
- [ ] Fire hydrant
- [ ] Fisherdog's catch
- [ ] 2 Golfers
- [ ] Guard
- [ ] Heart
- [ ] Heron
- [ ] High rise condos
- [ ] Human
- [ ] 3 Joggers
- [ ] 6 Limousines
- [ ] Periscope
- [ ] Pillow
- [ ] Pool
- [ ] Sipping a soda
- [ ] Star
- [ ] Tennis player
- [ ] TV antenna
- [ ] Umbrella
- [ ] Violinist
- [ ] Water-skier
- [ ] Whale

HUNT FOR HECTOR AT THE K-9 CLEANUP AND . . .

- ☐ Anchor
- ☐ Bath brush
- ☐ 3 Birds
- ☐ Bomb
- ☐ Broom
- ☐ 2 Burned out light bulbs
- ☐ Cannon
- ☐ Cat
- ☐ Coffin
- ☐ Dog bowl
- ☐ Doghouse
- ☐ Dog in disguise
- ☐ Elephant
- ☐ 4 Empty food cans
- ☐ 3 Fire hydrants
- ☐ Fire pig
- ☐ Fisherdog
- ☐ Flying fish
- ☐ Frankenswine
- ☐ Garbage can
- ☐ Horse
- ☐ Indian dog
- ☐ "K-8"
- ☐ Life preserver
- ☐ Lunch box
- ☐ Mermaid
- ☐ Mob spy
- ☐ Mouse
- ☐ Net
- ☐ Oil leak
- ☐ Old dog
- ☐ Old tire
- ☐ Palm tree
- ☐ Penguin
- ☐ Periscope
- ☐ Pighole cover
- ☐ Rabbit
- ☐ Rubber duck
- ☐ Sailor pig
- ☐ Skateboard
- ☐ Telescope
- ☐ Violin case

HUNT FOR HECTOR
AT THE SUPER
DOG BOWL
AND . . .

- ☐ "Almost
  Wet Paint"
- ☐ Arrow
- ☐ Beach ball
- ☐ Bird
- ☐ Bowling ball
- ☐ Cactus
- ☐ Candycane
- ☐ Cheerleaders
- ☐ Chicken
- ☐ Coach
- ☐ "Dog Aid"
- ☐ "Dogs U"
- ☐ Egg
- ☐ "Exit"
- ☐ 3 Flowers
- ☐ Ghost
- ☐ Heart
- ☐ Hobby horse
- ☐ Hot dog
- ☐ Megaphone
- ☐ "Mom"
- ☐ Mouse
- ☐ "No Barking"
- ☐ "Number 1"
- ☐ Paddleball
- ☐ Paintbrush
- ☐ 2 Pigs
- ☐ Pirate
- ☐ Propeller cap
- ☐ 5 Pumpkins
- ☐ Rabbit
- ☐ Skull and
  crossbones
- ☐ Super Bowl I
- ☐ Super Bowl II
- ☐ Super Bowl III
- ☐ Sword
- ☐ Tombstone
- ☐ Turtle
- ☐ TV camera
- ☐ TV set
- ☐ Water bucket
- ☐ "Wet Paint"
- ☐ Worm

HUNT FOR HECTOR AT THE DOG MALL AND . . .

HUNT FOR HECTOR
AT THE DOG
OLYMPICS AND . . .

- ☐ Archer
- ☐ 7 Arrows
- ☐ Basketball
- ☐ Batter
- ☐ Bomb
- ☐ Bone balloon
- ☐ Boomerang
- ☐ Broom
- ☐ Caddy
- ☐ Car chase
- ☐ Cyclers
- ☐ Dunce cap
- ☐ Fencers
- ☐ "Fetch"
- ☐ Football
- ☐ "Go Dogs"
- ☐ Golf ball
- ☐ Gymnasts
- ☐ "Hi, Mom"
- ☐ Hockey game
- ☐ Horse
- ☐ Horseshoe
- ☐ Ice cream cone
- ☐ Karate chop
- ☐ Lacrosse stick
- ☐ Paper plane
- ☐ Pole vaulter
- ☐ Rower
- ☐ Skateboard
- ☐ Skier
- ☐ 2 Sleeping dogs
- ☐ Snow dog
- ☐ Soccer ball
- ☐ Starter's gun
- ☐ "Stop"
- ☐ Target
- ☐ Trainer
- ☐ TV camera
- ☐ "Very Thin Ice"
- ☐ Weight lifter
- ☐ Yo-yo

HUNT FOR HECTOR
AT THE TV QUIZ
SHOW
AND . . .

- ☐ "Answer"
- ☐ Ape
- ☐ Astronaut
- ☐ Band
- ☐ Binoculars
- ☐ 2 Birds
- ☐ Candle
- ☐ Cap
- ☐ Cue cards
- ☐ Director
- ☐ Elephant
- ☐ Fairy dog
- ☐ Fire hydrant
- ☐ Flashlight
- ☐ Flowerpot
- ☐ Giant dog bowl
- ☐ Giraffe
- ☐ Gold bar
- ☐ Hot dogs
- ☐ "Howl"
- ☐ "Junk Food"
- ☐ King dog
- ☐ Leash
- ☐ "Let's Go Dogs"
- ☐ Lunch box
- ☐ 4 Microphones
- ☐ Mouse
- ☐ Oil can
- ☐ Party hat
- ☐ Pearls
- ☐ Photographer
- ☐ "Quiet"
- ☐ Ring
- ☐ Robot
- ☐ Sleeping dog
- ☐ Snowman
- ☐ Sock
- ☐ Steak
- ☐ Straw hat
- ☐ "Take 1"
- ☐ 5 TV cameras
- ☐ TV set
- ☐ "V.I.P. Room"

HUNT FOR HECTOR IN SPACE AND . . .

- ☐ Bark Vader
- ☐ Boat
- ☐ Boney Way
- ☐ Book
- ☐ Bow-wow land
- ☐ Boxing glove
- ☐ Cat
- ☐ Condo
- ☐ Dog catcher
- ☐ Dog graduate
- ☐ Dog trek
- ☐ Doggy bag
- ☐ Duck Rogers
- ☐ Emergency stop
- ☐ Fire hydrant
- ☐ Flying
  dog house
- ☐ Flying food dish
- ☐ Jail
- ☐ Kite
- ☐ Launch site
- ☐ Lost and found
- ☐ Mail carrier
- ☐ Map
- ☐ Moon dog
- ☐ "No Barking"
- ☐ Parachute
- ☐ Pirate
- ☐ Pizza
- ☐ Planet of
  the bones
- ☐ Planet of
  the dogs
- ☐ Police dog
- ☐ Pup tent
- ☐ Puppy trainer
- ☐ Robot dog
- ☐ Sleeping dog
- ☐ Space circus
- ☐ Surfboard
- ☐ Swimming pool
- ☐ Tire
- ☐ Unicycle
- ☐ Vampire dog
- ☐ Vanishing dog

HUNT FOR HECTOR IN DOGTOWN AND . . .

HUNT FOR HECTOR   SEARCH FOR SAM   FIND FREDDIE   LOOK FOR L

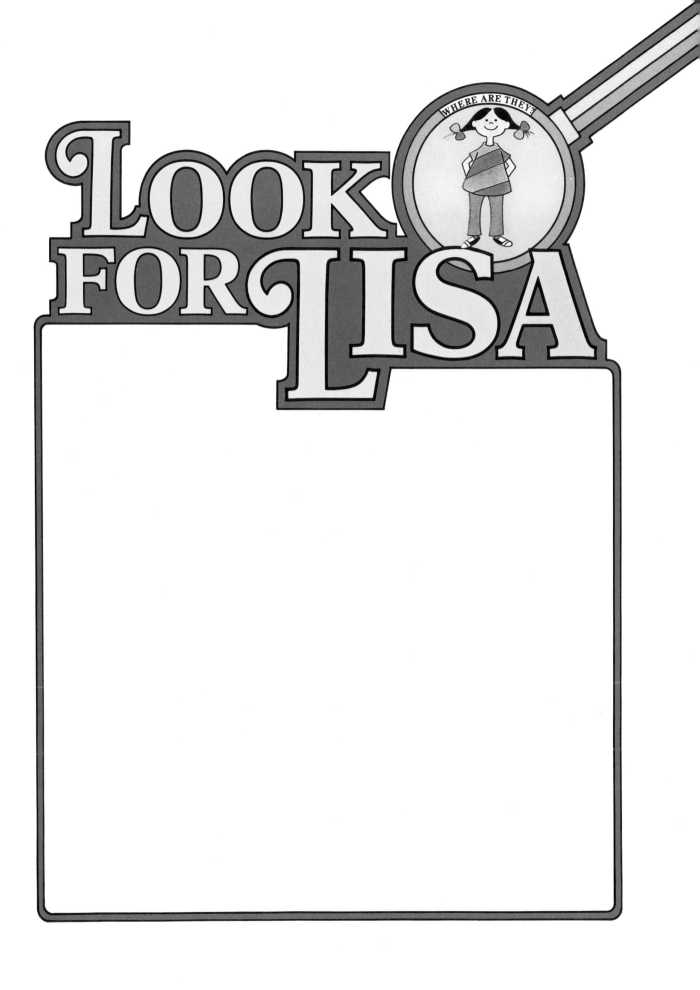

LOOK FOR LISA

WHERE ARE THEY?

LOOK FOR LISA AT THE MARATHON AND . . .

- ☐ Alien
- ☐ Alligator
- ☐ Ape
- ☐ Astronaut
- ☐ 2 Banana peels
- ☐ Barbell
- ☐ 5 Bats
- ☐ Big nose
- ☐ Cable car
- ☐ Cake
- ☐ Caveman
- ☐ 8 Chimneys
- ☐ Clown
- ☐ Convict
- ☐ Deep sea diver
- ☐ Drummer
- ☐ 2 Elephants
- ☐ Fire fighter
- ☐ Fish
- ☐ Flying carpet
- ☐ Football player
- ☐ Frankenstein monster
- ☐ Horse
- ☐ Ice skater
- ☐ Long-haired lady
- ☐ Man in a barrel
- ☐ Moose head
- ☐ Octopus
- ☐ Pig
- ☐ 6 Quitters
- ☐ Santa Claus
- ☐ Skier
- ☐ Sleeping jogger
- ☐ Snow White
- ☐ Tuba
- ☐ 2 Turtles
- ☐ Vampire
- ☐ Viking
- ☐ Waiter
- ☐ Worm

LOOK FOR LISA AFTER SCHOOL AND . . .

LOOK FOR LISA
AT THE ROCK
CONCERT AND . . .

- [ ] Alligator
- [ ] Apple
- [ ] Artist
- [ ] Beans
- [ ] Clown
- [ ] 2 Dogs
- [ ] Dwarf
- [ ] "Empty TV"
- [ ] Farmer
- [ ] Football player
- [ ] 4 Ghosts
- [ ] Giraffe
- [ ] 3 Guitars
- [ ] Heart
- [ ] 2 Hippos
- [ ] Hot dogs
- [ ] Hot foot
- [ ] Jogger
- [ ] Lamppost
- [ ] Lost balloon
- [ ] Magician
- [ ] "No Bus Stop"
- [ ] Pig
- [ ] Pink flamingo
- [ ] Pizza delivery
- [ ] Real cross wind
- [ ] Record albums
- [ ] Robot
- [ ] Rock
- [ ] Rock queen
- [ ] Roll
- [ ] Rooster
- [ ] Scarecrow
- [ ] School bus
- [ ] Skateboard
- [ ] 15 Speakers
- [ ] Stars
- [ ] Tent
- [ ] "Too Heavy
      Metal"
- [ ] Turtle
- [ ] Witch
- [ ] Zebra

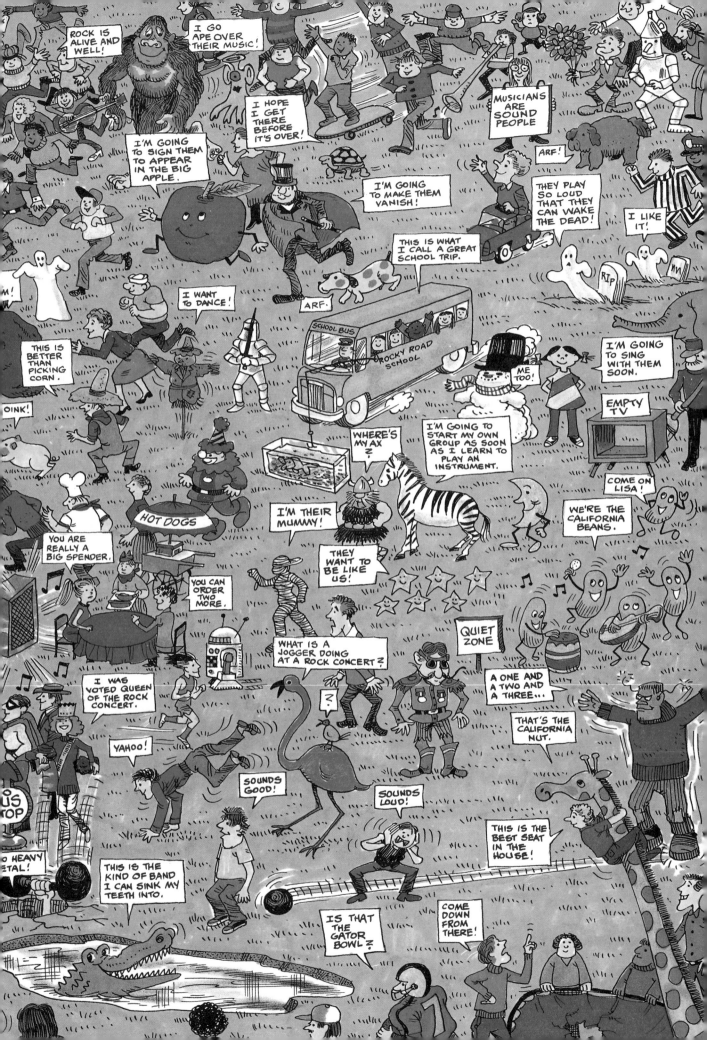

LOOK FOR LISA ON THE FARM AND . . .

LOOK FOR LISA AT THE BEACH AND . . .

- ☐ Artist
- ☐ Barrel of pickles
- ☐ Birdbath
- ☐ Boot
- ☐ 3 Bottles with notes
- ☐ Bubble gum
- ☐ 4 Cactuses
- ☐ 2 Clowns
- ☐ Cow
- ☐ Crocodile
- ☐ Dart thrower
- ☐ 4 Flying fish
- ☐ Hammerhead shark
- ☐ Leaking boat
- ☐ Lifesaver
- ☐ Litterbug
- ☐ Lost bathing suit
- ☐ 3 Mermaids
- ☐ Motorcyclist
- ☐ Mummy
- ☐ Musician
- ☐ Oil rig
- ☐ Pirate ship
- ☐ Polluted area
- ☐ 3 Radios
- ☐ Robinson Crusoe
- ☐ Rowboat
- ☐ Sailfish
- ☐ Seahorse
- ☐ Sea serpent
- ☐ Sleeping man
- ☐ Skull cave
- ☐ Stingray
- ☐ Submarine
- ☐ 6 Surfboards
- ☐ Telescope
- ☐ Thief
- ☐ Tricyclist
- ☐ Very quick sand
- ☐ 2 Water skiers

LOOK FOR LISA AT THE BIG SALE AND . . .

LOOK FOR LISA AROUND THE WORLD AND . . .

- ☐ Bear
- ☐ Big foot
- ☐ 2 Bridge builders
- ☐ Cactus
- ☐ Camel
- ☐ Cowboy
- ☐ Cup of coffee
- ☐ Cup of tea
- ☐ Dog
- ☐ Eskimo
- ☐ 12 Fish
- ☐ 2 Flying saucers
- ☐ Golfer
- ☐ Heart
- ☐ Ice castle
- ☐ Igloo
- ☐ Kangaroo
- ☐ Lighthouse
- ☐ Lion
- ☐ Mermaid
- ☐ Merman
- ☐ Oil well
- ☐ Ox
- ☐ 6 Penguins
- ☐ Rock singer
- ☐ 4 Sailboats
- ☐ Sea serpent
- ☐ 4 Skiers
- ☐ 2 Snowmen
- ☐ Stuck ship
- ☐ Submarine
- ☐ 3 Surfers
- ☐ Telescope
- ☐ 6 "Travel Agent" signs
- ☐ Tug boat
- ☐ T.V. set
- ☐ Unicorns in Utah
- ☐ Viking ship
- ☐ Walrus
- ☐ Whale

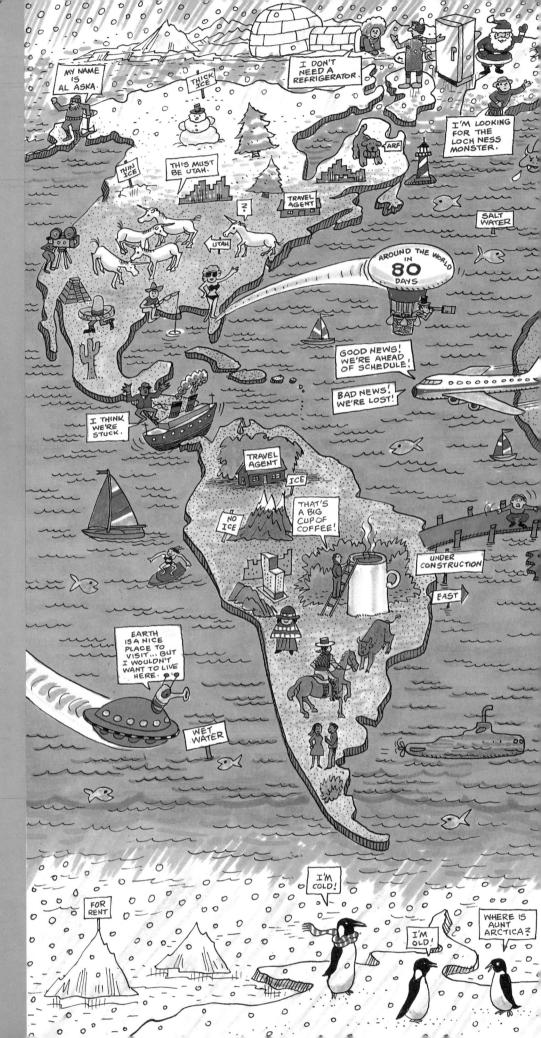

LOOK FOR LISA AT THE LIBRARY AND . . .

- ☐ Angel
- ☐ Banana peel
- ☐ Baseball cap
- ☐ Basketball players
- ☐ Book in a bottle
- ☐ 2 Bowling balls
- ☐ 4 Bullet holes
- ☐ Caveman
- ☐ Clown
- ☐ Copy machine
- ☐ 2 Cowboys
- ☐ Doctor
- ☐ Flying saucer
- ☐ Football
- ☐ Giant
- ☐ Hamburger
- ☐ Hammer
- ☐ Happy face
- ☐ 4 Hearts
- ☐ Hockey stick
- ☐ Horse
- ☐ Hula hoop
- ☐ Humpty Dumpty
- ☐ Moon
- ☐ Mummy and child
- ☐ Palm tree
- ☐ Paper plane
- ☐ 2 Parrots
- ☐ Pizza
- ☐ 7 "Quiet" signs
- ☐ 2 Radios
- ☐ Red wagon
- ☐ Referee
- ☐ Ship
- ☐ Skis
- ☐ 3 Skulls
- ☐ Telescope
- ☐ Tennis racket
- ☐ Tiny people
- ☐ TV camera
- ☐ Vacuum cleaner
- ☐ Worn tire

LOOK FOR LISA
AT THE
AMUSEMENT PARK
AND . . .

- ☐ Astronaut
- ☐ 15 Balloons
- ☐ Baseball
- ☐ Bomb
- ☐ Cactus
- ☐ Cheese
- ☐ Diplodocus
- ☐ "Do Not
   Read This"
- ☐ Entrance
- ☐ Exit
- ☐ Fishing hole
- ☐ 5 Ghosts
- ☐ Gorilla
- ☐ Graduate
- ☐ Headless man
- ☐ High diver
- ☐ Horse
- ☐ "Hot Dogs"
- ☐ "House Of
   Horrors"
- ☐ "Kisses"
- ☐ "Low Tide"
- ☐ 4 Mice
- ☐ 3 Monsters
- ☐ Mummy
- ☐ "No U-Turns"
- ☐ Pear
- ☐ Rocket
- ☐ Santa Claus
- ☐ "Scrambled
   Eggs"
- ☐ Skateboard
- ☐ Skull
- ☐ Snowman
- ☐ Thirteen
   o'clock
- ☐ Trash can
- ☐ Umbrella
- ☐ Vampire
- ☐ Witch

LOOK FOR LISA AT THE FLEA MARKET AND ...

- ☐ Ape
- ☐ Bag of peanuts
- ☐ Baseball cards
- ☐ Bathtub
- ☐ Bicycle
- ☐ 2 Bird cages
- ☐ Box of records
- ☐ 2 Cactuses
- ☐ Candle
- ☐ Clown doll
- ☐ Cowboy
- ☐ 2 Dogs
- ☐ Duck
- ☐ 3 Fish
- ☐ Flower
- ☐ Football
- ☐ 2 Frogs
- ☐ Garbage basket
- ☐ Gas mask
- ☐ Giant shoe
- ☐ Graduate
- ☐ Hammer
- ☐ Knight in armor
- ☐ Lamp shade
- ☐ Man in bottle
- ☐ 2 Men with fleas
- ☐ Monster hand
- ☐ Pearl necklace
- ☐ Piggy bank
- ☐ Potted palm plant
- ☐ Rocking chair
- ☐ Saddle
- ☐ Scoutmaster
- ☐ Smoke signals
- ☐ Spinning wheel
- ☐ Sunglasses
- ☐ Tennis racket
- ☐ Toy locomotive
- ☐ Trumpet
- ☐ Yo-yo

LOOK FOR LISA
AS THE CIRCUS
COMES TO TOWN
AND . . .

- ☐ Ape
- ☐ Baby carriage
- ☐ 6 Balloons
- ☐ 2 Batons
- ☐ Bird
- ☐ Cactus
- ☐ Camel
- ☐ Candle
- ☐ Cannon
- ☐ Cat
- ☐ 13 Clowns
- ☐ 8 Dogs
- ☐ 5 Elephants
- ☐ "Exit"
- ☐ "For Rent"
- ☐ Giraffe
- ☐ 5 Happy faces
- ☐ 2 Indians
- ☐ Jack-in-the-box
- ☐ 2 Keystone cops
- ☐ Lion
- ☐ 2 Martians
- ☐ "Not Wet Paint"
- ☐ Rabbit
- ☐ Super hero
- ☐ 7 Tents
- ☐ Ticket seller
- ☐ Tightrope
  walker
- ☐ Tin man
- ☐ Top hat
- ☐ Turtle
- ☐ 3 Umbrellas
- ☐ Unicycle
- ☐ Weightlifter
- ☐ Witch

LOOK FOR LISA   FIND FREDDIE   SEARCH FOR SAM   HUNT FOR HECT

SEARCH FOR SAM

WHERE ARE THEY?

SEARCH FOR SAM
IN CAT CITY AND . . .

- ☐ 2 Balloons
- ☐ Broken window
- ☐ Bus stop
- ☐ Car on sidewalk
- ☐ Catmobile
- ☐ Cat plane
- ☐ Clock
- ☐ Clown cat
- ☐ Cyclist
- ☐ "Do Not Litter"
- ☐ 2 Dogs
- ☐ Flat tire
- ☐ Flower pot
- ☐ Garbage truck
- ☐ 3 Ghost cats
- ☐ Human
- ☐ Ice skater
- ☐ Kite
- ☐ Kitty and
  Kats Avenues
- ☐ Locomotive
- ☐ 3 Mice
- ☐ Movie theater
- ☐ Penguin
- ☐ Piano
- ☐ Policecat
- ☐ Radio
- ☐ Roller skater
- ☐ Santa Claus
- ☐ Scarf
- ☐ 3 Sharks
- ☐ Ship on wheels
- ☐ 2 Skateboards
- ☐ Sleeping cat
- ☐ Sleigh
- ☐ Sock
- ☐ 5 Traffic
  accidents
- ☐ 8 Trash cans
- ☐ Waiter
- ☐ "What Time
  Is It?"
- ☐ Wind-up car

SEARCH FOR SAM AT THE FAT CAT HEALTH CLUB AND . . .

SEARCH FOR SAM AT THE MIDNIGHT MEOWING AND . . .

SEARCH FOR SAM
AT THE DISCO
AND . . .

- ☐ Ballerina
- ☐ 7 Balloons
- ☐ Break dancer
- ☐ Clown
- ☐ Cook
- ☐ Cowboy
- ☐ Dark glasses
- ☐ Disco duck
- ☐ Disco pig
- ☐ Dizzy cat
- ☐ Doctor
- ☐ Dog
- ☐ Duck
- ☐ Ear plugs
- ☐ Earrings
- ☐ Flower pot
- ☐ Hard hat
- ☐ Horn player
- ☐ Indian
- ☐ Karate cat
- ☐ Lamp shade
- ☐ 2 Mice
- ☐ Pig
- ☐ Pirate
- ☐ Pizza
- ☐ Police cat
- ☐ Rabbit
- ☐ Record eater
- ☐ Records
- ☐ 2 Rhinos
- ☐ Roller skates
- ☐ Scarf
- ☐ Skier
- ☐ Sleeping cat
- ☐ Snow cat
- ☐ 10 Speakers
- ☐ Swinging globe
- ☐ Top hat
- ☐ Record

SEARCH FOR SAM AT THE BATTLE OF CATS AND MICE AND . . .

- ☐ Banana peel
- ☐ Baseball
- ☐ Big cheese
- ☐ "Catnip"
- ☐ Catapult
- ☐ Cheese donut
- ☐ Chimney mouse
- ☐ Clock
- ☐ Condo
- ☐ 2 Cream pies
- ☐ Cup
- ☐ Dog
- ☐ Drummer
- ☐ Fake mouse
- ☐ 3 Fish
- ☐ Flower
- ☐ 'Fraidy cat
- ☐ Frankencat
- ☐ 4 Hearts
- ☐ Hobby horse
- ☐ Horn blower
- ☐ Hose
- ☐ Ink
- ☐ Judge
- ☐ Key
- ☐ Knapsack
- ☐ Light bulb
- ☐ Mask
- ☐ Monkey
- ☐ Mouse trap
- ☐ Owl
- ☐ 2 Pigs
- ☐ Quill pen
- ☐ Sleeping mouse
- ☐ Spider
- ☐ Sword
- ☐ Top hat
- ☐ Watering can
- ☐ Worm
- ☐ Yarn

SEARCH FOR SAM IN ANCIENT EGYPT AND . . .

SEARCH FOR SAM
AT THE CAT SHOW
AND . . .

- ☐ Banjo
- ☐ Beach chair
- ☐ Bird
- ☐ Black cat
- ☐ Cat costume
- ☐ Cat guard
- ☐ Cat in a hat
- ☐ Cat on a
  woman's head
- ☐ Clown
- ☐ Cow
- ☐ Curtain
- ☐ 2 Dogs
- ☐ Elephant
- ☐ Fat cat
- ☐ 2 Fish bowls
- ☐ Fishing pole
- ☐ Groucho cat
- ☐ Hobo cat
- ☐ Jogging cat
- ☐ 3 Judges
- ☐ Light bulb
- ☐ Lion
- ☐ "Moo Juice"
- ☐ Mouse
- ☐ Photographer
- ☐ Pizza
- ☐ Pool
- ☐ "Princess"
- ☐ Scaredy cat
- ☐ Scarf
- ☐ Scratching
  post
- ☐ Sombrero
- ☐ Sunglasses
- ☐ Telescope
- ☐ "The Real
  1st Prize"
- ☐ Tombstone
- ☐ Trombone
- ☐ "Wanted" poster
- ☐ Witch

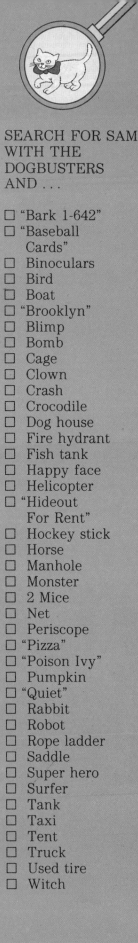

SEARCH FOR SAM
WITH THE
DOGBUSTERS
AND . . .

☐ "Bark 1-642"
☐ "Baseball
　　Cards"
☐ Binoculars
☐ Bird
☐ Boat
☐ "Brooklyn"
☐ Blimp
☐ Bomb
☐ Cage
☐ Clown
☐ Crash
☐ Crocodile
☐ Dog house
☐ Fire hydrant
☐ Fish tank
☐ Happy face
☐ Helicopter
☐ "Hideout
　　For Rent"
☐ Hockey stick
☐ Horse
☐ Manhole
☐ Monster
☐ 2 Mice
☐ Net
☐ Periscope
☐ "Pizza"
☐ "Poison Ivy"
☐ Pumpkin
☐ "Quiet"
☐ Rabbit
☐ Robot
☐ Rope ladder
☐ Saddle
☐ Super hero
☐ Surfer
☐ Tank
☐ Taxi
☐ Tent
☐ Truck
☐ Used tire
☐ Witch

SEARCH FOR SAM AT THE NORTH POLE AND ...

SEARCH FOR SAM   FIND FREDDIE   HUNT FOR HECTOR   LOOK FOR L